Arcimboldo's Portraits

Created by Claude Delafosse and Gallimard Jeunesse

MOONLIGHT
PUBLISHING

MY FIRST DISCOVERY PAPERBACKS

Come into the
imaginary world of a
most unusual painter,
Giuseppe Arcimboldo,
and discover his
amazing creations.

In this book, you
are able to look
at all the many
details and
brilliant colours of
his paintings.

Thanks to a simple torch
made of paper, you can
explore the dark pages
of this book.
It's like
magic!

You'll find the torch on the last page.
Press it out and slide it between the plastic
page and the black page underneath it.
You'll be amazed by what you light up!

Spring

A head made of flowers, a body all
of leaves, a collar of daisies,
that's Archimboldo's Spring.
Can you spot the little bell-like
flowers of the lily of the valley in
this magnificent bouquet?

As you move it around, you'll soon discover
all the details hidden in each picture.
When you have finished, put the torch
back in its pocket on the last page.

Giuseppe Arcimboldo was a painter
who lived during the Italian Renaissance.

He was born in Milan in 1527 and spent a large
part of his life at the courts in Vienna and Prague.
He painted very original portraits by placing
objects next to one another to form a face.

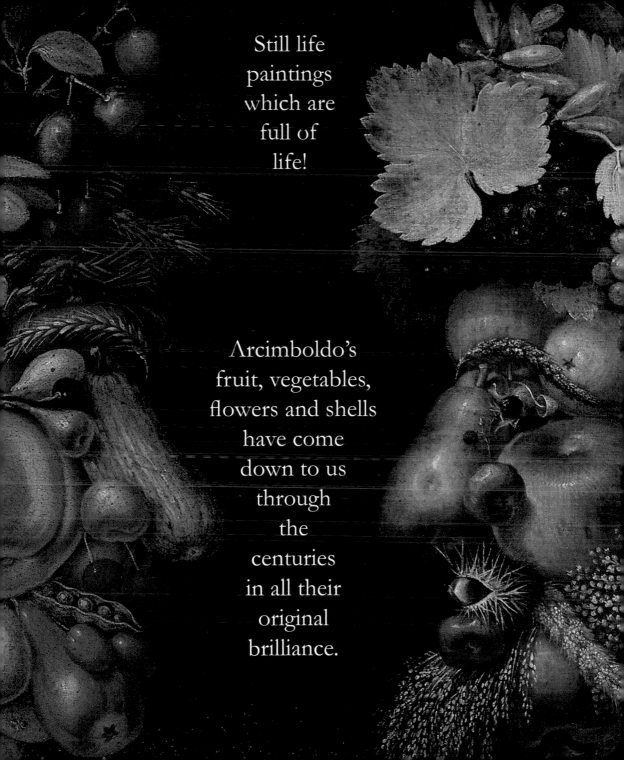

Still life
paintings
which are
full of
life!

Arcimboldo's
fruit, vegetables,
flowers and shells
have come
down to us
through
the
centuries
in all their
original
brilliance.

Spring

A head made of flowers, a body

all of leaves, a collar of daisies,

that's Arcimboldo's Spring.

Can you spot the little bell-like

flowers of the lily of the valley in

this magnificent bouquet?

Summer

A courgette for a nose,

a peach for a cheek,

cherries for lips, a pear for a chin;

that is how Arcimboldo paints

the portrait of Summer.

Can you find the ears of corn?

Autumn

A pear nose,

an apple cheek,

a sweet chestnut mouth,

an oaty beard

and grapes for hair;

Arcimboldo's Autumn is

dressed in an old barrel.

Can you see the snail?

Winter

A head of bark,

a mushroom mouth,

ivy for hair,

straw for clothes,

Arcimboldo's Winter sends a

cold shiver down your spine.

Thank goodness

for Spring!

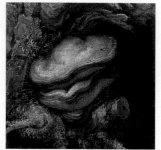

Water

Seawater or fresh water,

fish or shellfish...

Arcimboldo portrays water with

an unbelievable mixture of every

kind of water creature.

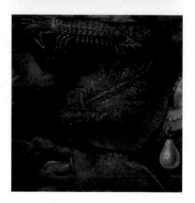

A cheek of hake, a shark for a

mouth, a crab shell for a breast

plate. Have you found the

seahorse?

Vertumnus-Rudolf II

Crowned with fruit,

wreathed in corn,

wearing a splendid sash

of flowers, this sumptuous

garden is sculpted

like an emperor. That is

how Arcimboldo portrays his

friend Prince Rudolf II

so magnificently.

The Librarian

Open books, closed books,

upright books, books leaning,

lying flat on their side, or piled

high; Arcimboldo has conjured

up an astonishing librarian.

Have you counted his paper

fingers?

The Gardener

A radish nose,

a mushroom mouth,

hazelnuts for eyes,

an onion cheek;

such is the Gardener

created by Arcimboldo.

Can you see him?

Turn the page upside down and

you will recognize him!

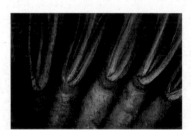

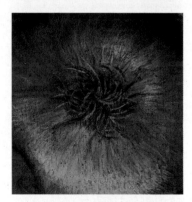

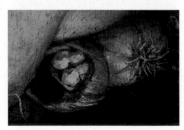

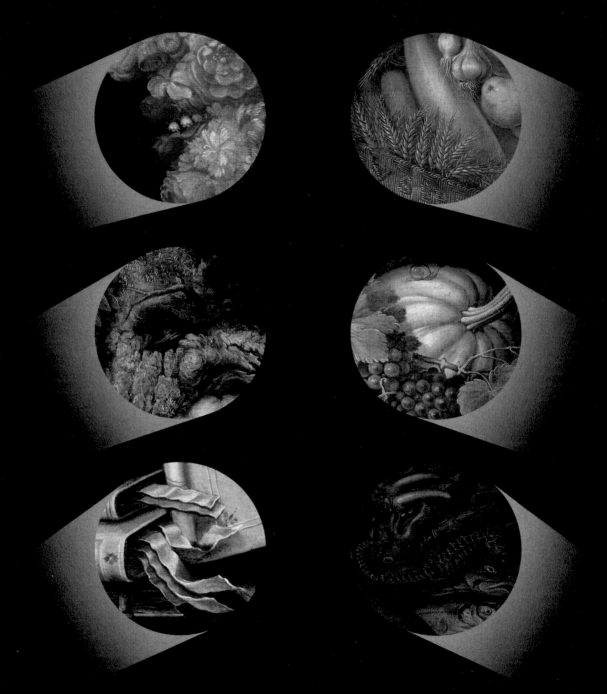

Can you find them using your magic torch?

MY FIRST DISCOVERY PAPERBACKS

Classics

Dinosaurs

The Egg

Farm Animals

Firefighting

Flowers

Fruit

Homes

The Jungle

Planes

The Seashore

The Town

Trains

Trees

Vegetables

Water

Torchlights

Animals Underground

Arcimboldo's Portraits

Insects

Inside the Body

Life below the City

Translated by Penelope Stanley-Baker
ISBN: 978-1-85103-752-0
© Éditions Gallimard Jeunesse, 1999.
English Text © Moonlight Publishing Ltd, 2022.
English audio rights ℗ Moonlight Publishing Ltd, 2022.
First published in the United Kingdom in 2022
by Moonlight Publishing Ltd,
2 Michael's Court, Hanney Road,
Southmoor, Oxfordshire, OX13 5HR
United Kingdom
Printed in China